A Fistful of Valuations

in the style of Warren Buffett and Charlie Munger

Second Edition, updated 2012

First Edition, Copyright © 2010

By Bud Labitan

All rights reserved.

Printed in the United States of America.

No part of this book may be used or reproduced

in any manner without permission.

ISBN: 978-1-105-95419-1

TABLE OF CONTENTS

INTRODUCTION

Chapter 1 : JEC, Jacobs Engineering Group Inc. 5/6/2010

Chapter 2 : JNJ, Johnson & Johnson 5/6/2010

Chapter 3 : MCK, McKesson Corp. 5/10/2010

Chapter 4 : TAP, Molson Coors Brewing Co. 5/9/2010

Chapter 5 : UNH, UnitedHealth Group Inc. 5/4/2010

Chapter 6 : The Four Filters

Chapter 7 : Preview of the new book, MOATS

INTRODUCTION

This book offers 5 sample "intrinsic value per share" business valuations in the style that Warren Buffett and Charlie Munger may use. In each case I tried to simulate an approach that they would take to valuing a business, based on what they have written and talked about. However, all of the growth assumptions used are my own. No consultation or endorsement was sought with Mr. Buffett or Mr. Munger. The examples given here are chosen for educational and illustrative purposes only. The valuation cases are estimations written in a style that emphasizes a focus on free cash flow and the number of shares outstanding. Readers are also encouraged to think about the business' competitive position. In reality, these businesses may outperform or they may underperform any of my projections.

This book is about five business cases from my Valuations book that looked like the most attractive bargains in 2010. I intentionally put a dull brown cover on the paperback and see if people would buy it.

I said then that folks could look at these five companies in 2015, and see how my predictions have worked out. Now in 2012, as I update this second edition and place it on the Amazon Kindle platform, I call your attention to a small flaw in the original valuation calculations done in 2010. They did not account for 10 "end of year" compounding periods. This has been corrected and the resulting "estimated intrinsic value estimations" are slightly lower, but not significantly different from those reported in 2010.

In this Second Edition, I corrected the "estimated intrinsic value estimations" calculations. However, I have not changed the text describing the business in 2010. This way the reader can see what I saw in 2010 and make their own judgments about the QB or Quality and Bargain within each business.

We can look at these five companies again in 2015, and see how my predictions have worked out.

Much of what I have learned has come from the letters of Warren Buffett to the shareholders of Berkshire Hathaway Inc. and the letters and speeches of Charlie Munger. In addition to each company's SEC filings, additional data used for these valuation cases came from multiple online sources that included: moneycentral.msn.com, finance.yahoo.com, wikinvest.com, google.com/finance, and morningstar.com

I tried to approach each valuation estimation without emotional bias. Any errors, assumptions, or omissions are my own. In reality, these businesses may outperform or they may underperform any of my projections.

How have my predictions or estimations done in two years? The results are seen in the table below. As of April 27, 2012 UNH, United Healthcare has gained the most in market value. It went from $29.49 to $57.91.

est. IV		May-10	4/27/2012	gain/loss
$61.76	JEC	$44.27	$44.60	$0.33
$80.60	JNJ	$63.40	$64.84	$1.44
$103.24	MCK	$66.49	$91.05	$24.56
$62.66	TAP	$41.96	$41.49	-$0.47
$61.97	UNH	$29.49	$57.91	$28.42

Interestingly, two of the medical industry businesses gained in market value while the remaining three businesses still seem to be in bargain territory. We shall see the five year results in 2015.

As a book, "Valuations" came about because I wanted a book that showed cases on how to sensibly value a business. The cases are full of warnings. For example, take a look at this statement: "Before we make a purchase decision, we must decide (filter #1) if XYZ business is a high quality business with good economics. Does XYZ business have (filter #2) enduring competitive advantages, and does XYZ business have (filter #3) honest and able management."

My first book, "The Four Filters Invention of Warren Buffett and Charlie Munger" talked about the thinking steps they perform in "framing and making" an investment decision. I came to the conclusion that the genius of Buffett and Munger's filtering process was to "capture all the important stakeholders" in a "multi-variable" process. Their rational approach captures Products, Enduring Customers, Managers, and Margin-of-Safety… all in one mixed "qualitative + quantitative" process.

In my view, their "decision framing process" was a remarkable advance in Behavioral Finance.

In the valuations book, I added some material about competitive advantages and competitive disadvantages, as well as their competitors. However, as far as the ability and trustworthiness of each businesses managers, I must leave this component of evaluation to you the reader. There are hints into their abilities and trustworthiness hidden in the past performance records and in their compensation numbers.

I hope you enjoy this shorter case book, and you benefit from the attempts made to advance our knowledge.

Bud Labitan

budlabitan@aol.com

Chapter 1

An estimated valuation of Jacobs Engineering Group Inc (JEC) 5/6/2010

Jacobs Engineering Group Inc. is a technical professional services firm in the United States. It provides a range of technical, professional, and construction services to industrial, commercial, and governmental clients globally. It provides four categories of services, including project services, which include engineering, design, architectural, and similar services; process, scientific and systems consulting services, which includes services performed in connection with a range of scientific testing, analysis, and consulting activities; construction services, which encompasses construction services, as well as modular construction activities, and includes direct-hire construction and construction management services, and operations and maintenance services, which includes services performed in connection with operating facilities on behalf of clients, as well as services involving process plant maintenance. In February 2010, the Company acquired Jordan, Jones and Goulding, Inc

Does JEC make for an intelligent investment or intelligent speculation today? Let us do a rough estimation of intrinsic value per share. Starting with a base estimate of annual Free Cash Flow at a value of approximately $400,000,000 and the number of shares outstanding at 125,000,000 shares; I used an assumed FCF annual growth of 11 percent for the first 10 years and assume zero growth from years 11 to

15. Review the Free Cash Flow record here, and think about its sustainability:

http://quicktake.morningstar.com/stocknet/CashFlowRatios10.aspx?Country=USA&Symbol=JEC&stocktab=keyratio

The resulting estimated intrinsic value per share (discounted back to the present) is approximately $61.76. Market Price = $44.27 Intrinsic Value = $61.76 (estimated)   Debt/Equity ratio = .03   Price To Value (P/V) ratio = .72 and the estimated bargain = 28. percent.

More importantly, before we make a purchase decision, we must decide (filter #1) if JEC is a high quality business with good economics. Does JEC have (filter #2) enduring competitive advantages, and does JEC have (filter #3) honest and able management. The current price/earnings ratio = 17.6 It 's current return on capital = 10.68

Using a debt to equity ratio of .03, JEC shows a 5-year average return on equity = 16.9

The biggest threat to profitability is: Competition and Economic Downturns. The main competitors are: Bechtel Group, Inc. (privately held), FLR = Fluor Corporation, FWLT = Foster Wheeler AG, Technical Services Industry.

The Main Competitive Advantage currently is: Ability to provide a broad range of technical, professional, and construction services to industrial, commercial, and governmental clients globally.

Further discussions on competitive pressures can be viewed here: http://www.wikinvest.com/stock/JEC

You the reader can insert your notes about management here:

Some industries have higher ROE because they require no assets, such as consulting firms. Other industries require large infrastructure builds before they generate a penny of profit, such as oil refiners. Generally, capital-intensive businesses have higher barriers to entry, which limit competition. But, high-ROE firms with small asset bases have lower barriers to entry. Thus, such firms face more business risk because competitors can replicate their success without having to obtain much outside funding.

Growth benefits investors only when the business in point can invest at incremental returns that are enticing; only when each dollar used to finance the growth creates over a dollar of long-term market value. In the case of a low-return business requiring incremental funds, growth hurts the investor. The wonderful companies sustain a competitive advantage, produce free cash flow, and use debt wisely.

Does JEC make for an intelligent investment or speculation today? Time is said to be the friend of the wonderful company and the enemy of the mediocre one. Before making an investment decision, seek understanding about the company, its products, and its sustainable competitive advantages over competitors. Next, look for able and trustworthy managers who are focused more on value than just growth.

Finally ask: *Is there a bargain relative to its intrinsic value per share today?*

Great investment opportunities come around when excellent companies are surrounded by unusual circumstances that cause the stock to be misappraised. In terms of Opportunity Cost, is JEC the best place to invest our money today? Or, are there better alternatives? How will JEC compete going forward? Technologies change and new technology can emerge. Keep in mind that a financial report like this is a reflection of the past and present. It may be used to project a future, but it may not account for factors yet unseen. Therefore, pay attention to competitive and market factors that may affect changes in profitability.

On May 19, 2010, Zacks Equity Research stated that Jacobs' track record of contract wins has encouraged analysts to raise their estimates. Further, Jacobs' high level of liquidity, with a net cash of $743 million, will help sustain JEC during these difficult market conditions.

In summary, using a debt to equity ratio of .03, JEC shows a 5-year average return on equity = 16.9 . Based on a holding and compounding period of 10 years, and a purchase price bargain of 28 percent, and a relative FCF growth of 11 percent, then the estimated effective annual yield on this investment may be greater than 14.3%. Going forward, are there any transformational catalysts or condition indicators imaginable on the horizon? Technologies change and new technologies will appear on the scene. Would brand loyalty keep customers buying here?

SEC Filings online:

http://www.sec.gov/cgi-bin/browse-edgar?company=&CIK=JEC&filenum=&State=&SIC=&owner=include&action=getcompany

Chapter 2

An estimated valuation of JNJ, Johnson & Johnson 5/6/2010

Johnson & Johnson is engaged in the research and development, manufacture and sale of a range of products in the health care field. The Company operates in three business segments: Consumer, Pharmaceutical, and Medical Devices and Diagnostics. In July 2009, Johnson & Johnson completed the acquisition of Cougar Biotechnology, Inc. with approximately 95.9% interest in Cougar Biotechnology's outstanding common stock. In September 2009, Elan Corporation, plc and Johnson & Johnson announced that JANSSEN Alzheimer Immunotherapy, a newly formed subsidiary of Johnson & Johnson, has completed the acquisition of substantially all of the assets and rights of Elan related to its Alzheimer`s Immunotherapy Program (AIP). In March 2010, Hypermarcas SA acquired 99.99% of Versoix Participacoes Ltda from the Company.

Last Price 63.40   52 Week High 66.20   52 Week Low 53.54

Does JNJ make for an intelligent investment or intelligent speculation today? Let us do a rough estimation of intrinsic value per share. Starting with a base estimate of annual Free Cash Flow at a value of approximately $14,000,000,000 and the number of shares outstanding at 2,758,000,000 shares; I used an assumed FCF annual growth of 8 percent for the first 10 years and assume zero growth from years 11 to

15. Review the Free Cash Flow record here, and think about its sustainability:

http://quicktake.morningstar.com/stocknet/CashFlowRatios10.aspx?Country=USA&Symbol=JNJ

Starting with an assumed FCF annual growth of 8 percent, the estimated intrinsic value per share is approximately $ 80.6 and you entered at a market price of $63.4 , so the P/V ratio = .79 and the estimated bargain = 21 percent. purchase price bargain of 21 percent, and a relative FCF growth of 8 percent, then the estimated effective annual yield may be greater than 10.4 %. The resulting estimated intrinsic value per share (discounted back to the present) is approximately $80.6.

Market Price = $63.4   Intrinsic Value = $80.6 (estimated)   Keep in mind, and compare that Coca Cola's Debt/Equity ratio is .47 or 47 percent; the Debt/Equity ratio here = na Price To Value (P/V) ratio = .79 and the estimated bargain = 21 percent.

More importantly, before we make a purchase decision, we must decide (filter #1) if JNJ is a high quality business with good economics. Does JNJ have (filter #2) enduring competitive advantages, and does JNJ have (filter #3) honest and able management. The current price/earnings ratio = 13.7 It 's current return on capital = 17.91

Using a debt to equity ratio of near zero, JNJ shows a 5-year average return on equity = 27.8

The biggest threat to profitability is: Competition and pricing.

The main competitors are: Abbott Laboratories, Amgen Inc., AstraZeneca PLC, Biogen Idec Inc., Bristol-Myers Squibb Company, Genentech, Inc., Genzyme Corp., Gilead Sciences Inc., GlaxoSmithKline plc, Johnson & Johnson, King Pharmaceuticals Inc., Life Technologies Corporation, MedImmune, L.L.C., Merck Serono S.A., Mylan, Inc., Novartis AG, Pfizer Inc., Ranbaxy Laboratories Limited, Sandoz International GmbH, Sanofi-Aventis, Teva Pharmaceutical Industries Limited, Watson Pharmaceuticals Inc.

The Main Competitive Advantage currently is: Johnson & Johnson is the world's second largest and most broadly based manufacturer of health care products. The company holds a significant share of the consumer and pharmaceutical markets. JNJ is also the world's largest developer and manufacturer of medical treatment and diagnostic devices. The consumer health market is expanding as consumers are taking greater responsibility and interest in their own health. Johnson & Johnson owns highly successful brands such as Tylenol, Band-Aid, and Neutrogena. The acquisition of Pfizer's Consumer Healthcare division in 2006 and addition of brands such as Listerine, Lubriderm, Visine, and Neosporin further solidified Johnson & Johnson dominance in consumer health care. Further discussions on competitive pressures can be viewed here: http://www.wikinvest.com/stock/JNJ

You the reader can insert your notes about management here:

Some industries have higher ROE because they require no assets, such as consulting firms. Other industries require large infrastructure builds before they generate a penny of profit, such as oil refiners. Generally, capital-intensive businesses have higher barriers to entry, which limit competition. But, high-ROE firms with small asset bases have lower barriers to entry. Thus, such firms face more business risk because competitors can replicate their success without having to obtain much outside funding.

Growth benefits investors only when the business in point can invest at incremental returns that are enticing; only when each dollar used to finance the growth creates over a dollar of long-term market value. In the case of a low-return business requiring incremental funds, growth hurts the investor. The wonderful companies sustain a competitive advantage, produce free cash flow, and use debt wisely.

Does JNJ make for an intelligent investment or speculation today? Time is said to be the friend of the wonderful company and the enemy of the mediocre one. Before making an investment decision, seek understanding about the company, its products, and its sustainable competitive advantages over competitors. Next, look for able and trustworthy managers who are focused more on value than just growth. Finally ask: *Is there a bargain relative to its intrinsic value per share today?*

Great investment opportunities come around when excellent companies are surrounded by unusual circumstances that cause the stock to be misappraised. In terms of Opportunity Cost, is JNJ the best place to invest our money today? Or, are there better alternatives? How will JNJ compete going forward? Technologies change and new technology can emerge. Keep in mind that a financial report like this is a reflection of the past and present. It may be used to project a future, but it may not account for factors yet unseen. Therefore, pay attention to competitive and market factors that may affect changes in profitability.

McNeil Consumer Healthcare, the JNJ subsidiary that makes Tylenol products, posted seven recall notices between September 2009 and March 2010. The company voluntary recalled 43 over-the-counter medicines, including liquid versions of Tylenol, Motrin, Zyrtec and Benadryl, because of "manufacturing deficiencies which may affect quality, purity or potency," according to the FDA. Those "manufacturing deficiencies" included manufacturing process, control, and procedure issues, such as inadequate laboratory facilities and untrained staff.

See the full article from DailyFinance:

http://www.dailyfinance.com/story/company-news/tylenol-recall-update/19483610/?icid=sphere_copyright

In summary, using a debt to equity ratio of near zero, JNJ shows a 5-year average return on equity = 27.8 . Based on a holding and compounding period of 10 years, and a purchase price bargain of 21.3 percent, and a relative FCF growth of 8 percent, then the estimated effective annual yield on this investment may be greater than 10.4%.

Going forward, are there any transformational catalysts or condition indicators imaginable on the horizon? Technologies change and new technologies will appear on the scene. Would brand loyalty keep customers buying here?

SEC Filings online: http://www.sec.gov/cgi-bin/browse-edgar?company=&CIK=JNJ&filenum=&State=&SIC=&owner=include&action=getcompany

Chapter 3

An estimated valuation of MCK, McKesson Corp. 5/10/2010

McKesson Corporation (McKesson) provides medicines, pharmaceutical supplies, information and care management products and services across the healthcare industry. The Company operates in two segments. The McKesson Distribution Solutions segment distributes ethical and drugs, medical-surgical supplies and equipment and health and beauty care products throughout North America. This segment also provides specialty pharmaceutical solutions for biotech and pharmaceutical manufacturers, sells financial, operational and clinical solutions for pharmacies (retail, hospital, long-term care) and provides consulting, outsourcing and other services. This segment includes a 49% interest in Nadro, S.A. de C.V. (Nadro), and a 39% interest in Parata Systems, LLC (Parata). The McKesson Technology Solutions segment delivers enterprise-wide clinical, patient care, financial, supply chain, strategic management and software solutions. This segment also includes its Payor group of businesses. Does MCK make for an intelligent investment or intelligent speculation today? Let us do a rough estimation of intrinsic value per share. Starting with a base estimate of annual Free Cash Flow at a value of approximately $2,137,000,000 and the number of shares outstanding at 271,000,000 shares; I used an assumed FCF annual growth of 5 percent for the first 10 years and assume zero growth from years 11 to

15. Review the Free Cash Flow record here, and think about its sustainability:

http://quicktake.morningstar.com/stocknet/CashFlowRatios10.aspx?Country=USA&Symbol=MCK

The resulting estimated intrinsic value per share (discounted back to the present) is approximately $103.24. Market Price = $66.49   Intrinsic Value = $103.24 (estimated)   Keep in mind, and compare that Coca Cola's Debt/Equity ratio is .47 or 47 percent; the Debt/Equity ratio here = .3 Price To Value (P/V) ratio = .64 and the estimated bargain = 35.6 percent.

More importantly, before we make a purchase decision, we must decide (filter #1) if MCK is a high quality business with good economics. Does MCK have (filter #2) enduring competitive advantages, and does MCK have (filter #3) honest and able management. The current price/earnings ratio = 13.8 It 's current return on capital = 12.11

Using a debt to equity ratio of .3, MCK shows a 5-year average return on equity = 15.5

The biggest threat to profitability is: Competition. The main competitors are: ABC = AmerisourceBergen Corporation, CAH = Cardinal Health, Inc., OMI = Owens & Minor Inc., Industry = Drugs Wholesale.

The Main Competitive Advantage currently is: McKesson (NYSE: MCK) is one of the world's largest corporations and the leading company in the $252 billion pharmaceutical distribution industry. McKesson also provides enterprise-level software solutions to hospitals and other healthcare organizations. In the past, McKesson operated on a buy/hold business model but recently shifted to a fee-for-service business model in order to eliminate the company's dependency for profit on drug price inflation.

Further discussions on competitive pressures can be viewed here: http://www.wikinvest.com/stock/MCK

You the reader can insert your notes about management here:

The shift from branded to generic drugs (as branded drugs lose their patents), allows distributors to benefit from both higher profit margins and higher total sales volume. Changes in health care policy, especially Medicare, can result in a larger volume of drugs being purchased, but threaten profits with cost controlling and transparency. As the U.S. population grows older, there will be a higher demand for pharmaceuticals. There is also the longer-term threat that providers and manufactures may one day be able to cut out the middlemen distributors.

McKesson has diversified outside of pharmaceutical and medical supplies businesses through its healthcare software and information technology offerings. Although this segment accounts for only approximately 2% of McKesson's revenue currently, it is by far McKesson's most profitable business. The market for healthcare IT is large and fragmented. The top 17 firms in the healthcare IT industry hold only approximately 40% of the market. Therefore, there is potential for McKesson to build on its leading market share in this high-margin sector.

Some industries have higher ROE because they require no assets, such as consulting firms. Other industries require large infrastructure builds before they generate a penny of profit, such as oil refiners. Generally, capital-intensive businesses have higher barriers to entry, which limit competition. But, high-ROE firms with small asset bases have lower barriers to entry. Thus, such firms face more business risk because competitors can replicate their success without having to obtain much outside funding.

Growth benefits investors only when the business in point can invest at incremental returns that are enticing; only when each dollar used to finance the growth creates over a dollar of long-term market value. In the case of a low-return business requiring incremental funds, growth hurts the investor. The wonderful companies sustain a competitive advantage, produce free cash flow, and use debt wisely.

Does MCK make for an intelligent investment or speculation today? Time is said to be the friend of the wonderful company and the enemy of the mediocre one. Before making an investment decision, seek understanding about the company, its products, and its sustainable competitive advantages over competitors. Next, look for able and trustworthy managers who are focused more on value than just growth. Finally ask: *Is there a bargain relative to its intrinsic value per share today?*

Great investment opportunities come around when excellent companies are surrounded by unusual circumstances that cause the stock to be misappraised. In terms of Opportunity Cost, is MCK the best place to invest our money today? Or, are there better alternatives? How will MCK compete going forward? Technologies change and new technology can emerge. Keep in mind that a financial report like this is a reflection of the past and present. It may be used to project a future, but it may not account for factors yet unseen. Therefore, pay attention to competitive and market factors that may affect changes in profitability.

A May 19th report from DOW JONES NEWSWIRES states that the Moody's Investors Service placed its near-junk ratings on McKesson Corp. (MCK) on watch for upgrade, citing the distributor of pharmaceutical products' improved margins in both its distribution and information-systems segments. Moody's rating on McKesson stands at Baa3, which is one notch into investment-grade territory.

In summary, using a debt to equity ratio of .3, MCK shows a 5-year average return on equity = 15.5 .

Based on a holding and compounding period of 10 years, and a purchase price bargain of 35.6 percent, and a relative FCF growth of 5 percent, then the estimated effective annual yield on this investment may be greater than 9.6%.

Going forward, are there any transformational catalysts or condition indicators imaginable on the horizon? Technologies change and new technologies will appear on the scene. Would brand loyalty keep customers buying here?

SEC Filings online: http://www.sec.gov/cgi-bin/browse-edgar?company=&CIK=MCK&filenum=&State=&SIC=&owner=include&action=getcompany

Chapter 4

An estimated valuation of Molson Coors Brewing Co., TAP 5/9/2010

Molson Coors Brewing Company (MCBC) is a holding company. Its operating subsidiaries include Coors Brewing Company (CBC), operating in the United States prior to the formation of MillerCoors LLC (MillerCoors); Molson Coors Brewing Company (UK) Limited (MCBC-UK), operating in the United Kingdom; Molson Coors Canada (MCC), operating in Canada, and other corporate entities. The Company operates in four segments: Canada, the United States, the United Kingdom and Molson Coors International (MCI). MCBC has a portfolio of more than 65 strategic and partner brands, including signature brands Coors Light, Molson Canadian and Carling, which are positioned to meet a range of consumer segments and occasions.

52 Week High 51.33   52 Week Low 38.44

Does TAP make for an intelligent investment or intelligent speculation today? Let us do a rough estimation of intrinsic value per share. Starting with a base estimate of annual Free Cash Flow at a value of approximately $730,000,000 and the number of shares outstanding at 185,000,000 shares; I used an assumed FCF annual growth of 8 percent for the first 10 years and assume zero growth from years 11 to 15. Review the Free Cash Flow record here, and think about its sustainability:

http://quicktake.morningstar.com/stocknet/CashFlowRatios10.aspx?Country=USA&Symbol=TAP

The resulting estimated intrinsic value per share (discounted back to the present) is approximately $62.66.

Market Price = $41.96   Intrinsic Value = $62.66 (estimated)   Keep in mind, and compare that Coca Cola's Debt/Equity ratio is .47 or 47 percent; the Debt/Equity ratio here = .24 Price To Value (P/V) ratio = .64 and the estimated bargain = 33 percent.

More importantly, before we make a purchase decision, we must decide (filter #1) if TAP is a high quality business with good economics. Does TAP have (filter #2) enduring competitive advantages, and does TAP have (filter #3) honest and able management. The current price/earnings ratio = 11. It 's current return on capital = 7.31

Using a debt to equity ratio of .24, TAP shows a 5-year average return on equity = 7.8

The biggest threat to profitability is: Competitive substitutes and competitor pricing. The main competitors are: The Coca-Cola Company, Pepsico, Inc. PEP, Dr Pepper Snapple Group, Inc. DPS, Groupe Danone World Water Division, Nestlé Waters Private, ITO EN, LTD. Private, Red Bull GmbH Private, Cott Corporation COT, BTVCF.PK, Ocean Spray Cranberries, Inc. Private, NSRGY.PK, Diageo plc DEO, HINKY.PK, SBMRY.PK, Anheuser-Busch InBev BUD, Suntory International Corp.

Private, Kraft Foods Inc. KFT, Pernod Ricard SA Private, GPMCF.PK, Constellation Brands Inc. STZ.

The Main Competitive Advantage currently is: Coors and Molson brands. Formed by the merger of the Coors Brewing Company and the Molson Company in 2005, the Molson Coors Brewing Company is the fifth largest brewer in the world by production volume. The company brews and sells 40 different beer products.

Further discussions on competitive pressures can be viewed here: http://www.wikinvest.com/stock/TAP

You the reader can insert your notes about management here:

Molson Coors was created when the Coors Brewing Company of America merged with Molson Canada on February 9, 2005. In 2007, the company announced a joint venture with SABMiller (SAB-LN). The deal, forming the second largest brewer in the US, after Anheuser-Busch Companies (BUD), was completed on July 1, 2008. Under the agreement, Molson Coors claims a 42% share in the joint venture's profits, but retains 50% voting rights. The joint venture only encompasses the company's operations in the US; its Canadian and UK businesses remain completely under the control of Molson Coors. The combined company benefits greatly from logistical and transportation synergies. Instead of having to brew Coors Light in Colorado and shipping it to the east coast, Molson Coors can now brew the beer in SABMiller (SAB-LN)'s east coast breweries, creating a simpler distribution chain. The company expects to realize cost savings of $500 million. Molson Coors, TAP, must maintain

Brand Loyalty in a highly competitive environment. TAP must also adapt to an increasingly consolidated beverage industry.

Some industries have higher ROE because they require no assets, such as consulting firms. Other industries require large infrastructure builds before they generate a penny of profit, such as oil refiners. Generally, capital-intensive businesses have higher barriers to entry, which limit competition. But, high-ROE firms with small asset bases have lower barriers to entry. Thus, such firms face more business risk because competitors can replicate their success without having to obtain much outside funding.

Growth benefits investors only when the business in point can invest at incremental returns that are enticing; only when each dollar used to finance the growth creates over a dollar of long-term market value. In the case of a low-return business requiring incremental funds, growth hurts the investor. The wonderful companies sustain a competitive advantage, produce free cash flow, and use debt wisely.

Does TAP make for an intelligent investment or speculation today? Time is said to be the friend of the wonderful company and the enemy of the mediocre one. Before making an investment decision, seek understanding about the company, its products, and its sustainable competitive advantages over competitors. Next, look for able and trustworthy managers who are focused more on value than just growth. Finally ask: *Is there a bargain relative to its intrinsic value per share today?*

Great investment opportunities come around when excellent companies are surrounded by unusual circumstances that cause the stock to be misappraised. In terms of Opportunity Cost, is TAP the best place to invest our money today? Or, are there better alternatives? How will TAP compete going forward? Technologies change and new technology can emerge. Keep in mind that a financial report like this is a reflection of the past and present. It may be used to project a future, but it may not account for factors yet unseen. Therefore, pay attention to competitive and market factors that may affect changes in profitability.

On May 03, 2010, BUSINESS WIRE reported that the Molson Coors Brewing Company announced that its Board of Directors has increased the quarterly dividend on its Class A and Class B common shares by 16.7 percent, or $0.04, to US$0.28 per share. This is equivalent to an annual dividend of US$1.12 per share, up from US$0.96. The dividend declaration is payable June 15, 2010, to shareholders of record as of May 28, 2010.

In summary, using a debt to equity ratio of .24, TAP shows a 5-year average return on equity = 7.8 . Based on a holding and compounding period of 10 years, and a purchase price bargain of 33. percent, and a relative FCF growth of 8 percent, then the estimated effective annual yield on this investment may be greater than 12.1%. Going forward, are there any transformational catalysts or condition indicators imaginable on the horizon? Technologies change and new technologies will appear on the scene. Would brand loyalty keep customers buying here?

SEC Filings online:

http://www.sec.gov/cgi-bin/browse-edgar?company=&CIK=TAP&filenum=&State=&SIC=&owner=include&action=getcompany

Chapter 5

An estimated valuation of UnitedHealth Group Inc. UNH 5/4/2010

UnitedHealth Group Incorporated (UnitedHealth Group) is a diversified health and well-being company. The Company operates in four business segments: Health Benefits, which includes UnitedHealthcare, Ovations and AmeriChoice; OptumHealth; Ingenix and Prescription Solutions. On June 1, 2009, the Company completed the acquisition of AIM Healthcare Services, Inc. (AIM). In March 2010, the Company acquired QualityMetric Incorporated.

Last Price 29.49   52 Week High 36.07   52 Week Low 22.80

Does UnitedHealth Group make for an intelligent investment or intelligent speculation today? Let us do a rough estimation of intrinsic value per share. Starting with a base estimate of annual Free Cash Flow at a value of approximately $4,800,000,000 and the number of shares outstanding at 1,153,000,000 shares; I used an assumed FCF annual growth of 7 percent for the first 10 years and assume zero growth from years 11 to 15. Review the Free Cash Flow record here, and think about its sustainability:

http://quicktake.morningstar.com/stocknet/CashFlowRatios10.aspx?Country=USA&Symbol=UNH

The resulting estimated intrinsic value per share (discounted back to the present) is approximately $61.97.

Market Price = $29.49   Intrinsic Value = $61.97 (estimated)   Keep in mind, and compare that Coca Cola's Debt/Equity ratio is .47 or 47 percent; the Debt/Equity ratio here = .47   Price To Value (P/V) ratio = .45 and the estimated bargain = 52 percent.

More importantly, before we make a purchase decision, we must decide (filter #1) if UNH is a high quality business with good economics. Does UNH have (filter #2) enduring competitive advantages, and does UNH have (filter #3) honest and able management. The current price/earnings ratio = 9.5 It 's current return on capital = 10.55

Using a debt to equity ratio of .47, UnitedHealth Group shows a 5-year average return on equity = 19.3

The biggest threat to profitability is: Competition and Government regulations that impose additional costs. The main competitors are: WellPoint Health Networks (WLP), Aetna (AET), Health Care Service Corporation, Humana (HUM), CIGNA Corporation (CI), Kaiser Permanente, Highmark, Inc., Blue Cross Blue Shield of Michigan, HIP Health Plan of New York, Centers for Medicare & Medicaid Services Private, Blue Cross and Blue Shield Association Private, UK National Health Service Private, Medco Health Solutions, Inc. Private, Caremark Pharmacy Services Private.

The Main Competitive Advantage currently is: The company generates 90% of its revenues through three health insurance organizations: one for private clients, one for Medicare recipients, and one for Medicaid beneficiaries. The government-sponsored clients represent an important source of business for UNH, so government can significantly impact United's profitability.

Further discussions on competitive pressures can be viewed here: http://www.wikinvest.com/stock/UNH

You the reader can insert your notes about management here:

United has a number of other products and services. Ingenix is a data gathering and analysis division. United uses the data to evaluate the effectiveness of its doctors and hospitals. UNH sells this information to other health industry professionals.

Some industries have higher ROE because they require no assets, such as consulting firms. Other industries require large infrastructure builds before they generate a penny of profit, such as oil refiners. Generally, capital-intensive businesses have higher barriers to entry, which limit competition. But, high-ROE firms with small asset bases have lower barriers to entry. Thus, such firms face more business risk because competitors can replicate their success without having to obtain much outside funding.

Growth benefits investors only when the business in point can invest at incremental returns that are enticing; only when each dollar used to finance the growth creates over a dollar of long-term market value. In the case of a low-return business requiring incremental funds, growth hurts the investor. The wonderful companies sustain a competitive advantage, produce free cash flow, and use debt wisely.

Does UnitedHealth Group make for an intelligent investment or speculation today? Time is said to be the friend of the wonderful company and the enemy of the mediocre one. Before making an investment decision, seek understanding about the company, its products, and its sustainable competitive advantages over competitors. Next, look for able and trustworthy managers who are focused more on value than just growth. Finally ask: *Is there a bargain relative to its intrinsic value per share today?*

Great investment opportunities come around when excellent companies are surrounded by unusual circumstances that cause the stock to be misappraised. In terms of Opportunity Cost, is UNH the best place to invest our money today? Or, are there better alternatives? How will UnitedHealth Group compete going forward? Technologies change and new technology can emerge. Keep in mind that a financial report like this is a reflection of the past and present. It may be used to project a future, but it may not account for factors yet unseen. Therefore, pay attention to competitive and market factors that may affect changes in profitability.

On Apr 27, 2010, BUSINESS WIRE reported that the UnitedHealthcare company has been selected to administer Colorado state's self-funded health insurance plans, which are offered to about 32,000 Colorado state employees and their families. The five-year contract is effective July 1, 2010.

In summary, using a debt to equity ratio of .47, UnitedHealth Group shows a 5-year average return on equity = 19.3 . Based on a holding and compounding period of 10 years, and a purchase price bargain of 52.4 percent, and a relative FCF growth of 7 percent, then the estimated effective annual yield on this investment may be greater than 14.6%. Going forward, are there any transformational catalysts or condition indicators imaginable on the horizon? Technologies change and new technologies will appear on the scene. Would brand loyalty keep customers buying here?

SEC Filings online: http://www.sec.gov/cgi-bin/browse-edgar?company=&CIK=UNH&filenum=&State=&SIC=&owner=include&action=getcompany

Chapter Six: The Four Filters

I believe that Warren Buffett and Charlie Munger invented an investing formula that is underappreciated by the business and academic communities. The Four Filters process functions as an effective time-tested focusing formula for investing success. They serve as a very useful guide for assessing intrinsic value and sensible price.

Behavioral Finance and Common Sense have shown us that we all have human tendencies to frame ideas that are affected by our emotions. Ideally, we would use the best of our emotional and intellectual energies in the right way.

Charlie Munger has spoken about the merits of having a "pilot's checklist." Warren Buffett mentioned the Filters in the 2007 annual report this way: "Charlie and I look for companies that have a) a business we understand; b) favorable long-term economics; c) able and trustworthy management; and d) a sensible price tag." These Four Filters can enhance the probability of our investment success. They will help you in your search for intrinsic value and sensible investment.

Warren Buffett learned from Ben Graham that the key to successful investing was the purchase of shares in good businesses when market prices were at a large discount from underlying business values. Along the way, he and Charlie Munger got better at picking stocks and whole companies for investment.

Note that growth is only one component in assessing value. Through the conscientious process of Elaboration and Elimination, the Filters illuminate the most important factors for business and investing success. The Filters highlight and reveal the good prospects and eliminate the bad prospects for investment. They encompass four clusters that are vitally important to investing success: 1. Products   2. Customers   3. Management 4. Margin of Safety.

If Buffett and Munger had focused solely on the fourth filter, "Margin of Safety" from bargain prices, they would have still done well. However, used as a sequential set of filters, the Four Filters are remarkably effective in preventing loss. It is an elegant algorithm that combines the use of important qualitative and quantitative decision steps. And, practicing these steps will make you a better investment thinker.

From a practical point of view, business is about taking good care of your customer and arriving at an agreeable trade. Finding the company that has enduring competitive advantage means that you are finding a business that has been tested by time and its customers. Products, Customers, Good Management, and Financial Safety given by a bargain purchase are always important. However, Charlie Munger has said that "people calculate too much and think too little." Here, the filters guide our thinking on a sequential path to understanding.

Within that Fourth Filter, Bargain Price, we see Ben Graham's three most important words in investing, "Margin of Safety." Investing safety is practically insured by purchasing at a bargain price.

This process can help us impose a greater prudence upon our investment decision making. Writing about speculation, Ben Graham believed that the value of analysis diminishes as the element of chance increases. However, if we decrease the element of chance, imagine what this does for our predictive probabilities.

By studying business situations more rationally, we can improve our decision making skills. Using the Filters, we can decrease the element of chance and increase our probability of focusing and finding a higher quality bargain.

Preview of Bud Labitan's new book.

Introduction Section Of "MOATS"

GOALS

Moats is designed to be a valuable learning resource for investors, students, and managers of business. It can also be used as a starting point for discussions about real competitive advantages in business schools around the world. This book is about the competitive advantages of 70 selected businesses that Warren Buffett and Charlie Munger bought for Berkshire Hathaway. (NYSE: BRK.A, BRK.B). Most of these businesses are wholly owned subsidiaries. A handful of them are partially owned through large stock (equity) investments.

Imagine these competitive advantages as protective moats around each economic castle. Will these economic moats endure over time? Over time, each customer makes up a part of that answer. Charlie Munger stated it this way: "How do you compete against a true fanatic? You can only try to build the best possible moat and continuously attempt to widen it."

DEFINITION OF MOATS

Moats are barriers. One of the oldest moats surrounded the ancient Egyptian settlement of Buhen, on the West bank of the Nile River.

During the medieval period, the kings of Europe would build wide and deep trenches filled with water around their castles. These moats were built as single or double protective barriers against invading armies. In business, we think of economic barriers that can both defend and injure the invading competition.

When I started this project, I searched the internet for images of castles with moats. Interestingly, I learned of Berkhamsted Castle and its double moat. (http://www.berkhamsted-castle.org.uk) The Castle remains are located about 20 miles northwest from the center of London, at Brownlow Road, Hertfordshire, Berkhamsted, United Kingdom.

Charlie Munger said, "Let's go for the wonderful business." So, after years of buying "bargain-purchase" follies, Warren Buffett and Charlie Munger realized that it is much better to buy a wonderful company at a fair price than a fair company at a wonderful price. Now, when buying companies or common stocks, they look for first-class businesses accompanied by first-class managements.

What makes a first-class business wonderful? It must have one or more economic moats. Charlie Munger observed that capitalism is a pretty brutal place. Yet, some good businesses can survive a little period of bad management. Warren Buffett said "A truly great business must have an enduring 'moat' that protects excellent returns on invested capital."

WHY THESE 70 BUSINESSES?

This book is about the competitive advantages of 70 of the many businesses that Warren Buffett and Charlie Munger bought for Berkshire Hathaway. Why did I focus on these 70? I took the names of the businesses listed on Berkshire Hathaway's website and its link to its subsidiaries. Then I added a few of their largest stock investments. They are arranged alphabetically. My intent was to study the economic moats, learn more about them, and see which ones are growing and which ones are shrinking.

SOURCES OF INFORMATION

The information comes from multiple online sources. The most important sources come from each business' publications and the annual letters of Warren Buffett to the shareholders of Berkshire Hathaway. Charlie Munger's letters and talks were also a great source of material. Other pieces of information were found by the many volunteers and students listed in the Appendix.

THANKS TO RESEARCH CONTRIBUTORS AND EDITORS

The research volunteers and contributors to this book were asked two basic questions. First, what are the competitive advantages of the business you are looking at? Secondly, are these advantages sustainable for the next ten years?

When I posted this offer out on the web, I was pleased to welcome many enthusiastic and knowledgeable volunteers. While much of my research was already compiled, I needed to test my ideas against someone else. This testing of ideas yielded additional information that was new and valuable. It resulted in a bigger, but also better book. So, I thank each and every one of the contributors listed in the Appendix and at the Moats website here: http://www.frips.com/book.htm

I extend a special thanks to Professor Phani Tej Adidam, Ph.D. who is the Executive Education Professor of Business Administration, and Chair, Department of Marketing and Management, and Director, CBA International Initiatives at University of Nebraska at Omaha. Professor Adidam's MBA students of 2011 have contributed valuable ideas to many of these chapters.

Thank you Richard Konrad, CFA, of Value Architects Asset Management. Rick has been an insightful contributor to several chapters. Thank you Dr. Maulik Suthar of Gujarat, India. Maulik has been a thoughtful contributor to several chapters, and an enthusiastic supporter of this project. Thank you Scott Thompson, MBA for sharing your thoughts, analysis, and feedback.

SINGLE, DOUBLE, AND TRIPLE MOATS

Having a "Sustainable Competitive Advantage" means customers keep coming back to repurchase. The two major areas of competitive advantage are: 1. a cost advantage, and 2. a differentiation advantage. While the "marketing mix" teaches us to think about the product, price, place, and promotions, this all comes together in the mind of the potential customer. The customer may or may not perceive these two general areas of advantage. This book refers to them as a "cost" and "special" advantages. I simplify by substituting the word "special" for differentiation.

Over the years, Warren Buffett and Charlie Munger found wonderful businesses by asking a lot of questions. What is the nature of each business? Can we predict it with a high degree of accuracy? Can we imagine a moat around each economic castle? Will this moat be enduring? Is there something special here for our customers, or is this advantage eroding?

Since the nature of capitalism is competition, a successful business needs to have "something special" in order to lead the pack and fend off present and potential competitors. It needs a barrier to entry. Sustainable Competitive Advantage is also called "favorable long-term prospects" or "enduring economic advantages." It comes from things that make a business difficult to copy or enter.

A brand is such a barrier because it represents something unique and valued in the mind of a customer that promotes customer loyalty. A valuable patent or trademark can also give a business a period of protected advantage, acting as a barrier to entry.

Warren Buffett and Charlie Munger added to Ben Graham's foundation of bargain hunting by looking for a business with a big protective moat around it. Buffett and Munger look for something special in peoples' minds such as: Lower Cost of Production, Brands, Economies of Scale, Patented Technology, Location, Distribution System, Specialized Services, Network, Regional Monopolies and Intangible Assets that create higher switching costs and a barrier to entry.

So what makes one business thrive better than another business? There must be something special. In one example, Charlie Munger recommended the autobiography of Les Schwab "Les Schwab Pride in Performance: Keep It Going." According to Munger, "Schwab ran tire shops in the Midwest and made a fortune by being shrewd in a tough business by having good systems." That was Schwab's specialty.

At GEICO insurance, the cost advantage present is a barrier for competitors. Can they match GEICO in cost or service? Buffett stated that GEICO's direct marketing gave it an enormous cost advantage over competitors that sold through agents. What about size and capital rating? GEICO certainly has strong backing, and Berkshire Hathaway's other insurance and reinsurance operations also benefit from the size, rating, and "time tested" operational soundness of its business organization.

This ability to endure over time, in good times and in bad, and continue to earn a solid profit is an important competitive advantage that helps make a company a "wonderful business." Sometimes, that comes about because of decent economics plus superior managements who work to build a stronger moat in the product or service by creating a special "brand" impression.

Talking about less competitive and weaker businesses, Warren Buffett said, "In many industries, differentiation simply can't be made meaningful. A few producers in such industries may consistently do well if they have a cost advantage that is both wide and sustainable." However, these are a few exceptional businesses. In many industries, such enduring winners do not exist. So, for the great majority of businesses selling "commodity" products, Buffett believes that a depressing equation of poor business economics prevails. In his view, "a persistent over-capacity without administered prices (or costs) equals poor profitability."

Buffett and Munger like strong brands like those of Coke, Gillette, and Kraft. These companies have increased their worldwide shares of market in recent years. Their brand names, the attributes of their products, and the strength of their distribution systems gives them competitive advantage. So what does this sustainable competitive advantage look like in numbers? Take a look at their 5-10 year records of FCF (Free Cash Flow) and real owner earnings compared to those of competing businesses.

Consider why the Coca-Cola Company is such a good business from an investor's point of view. Both Coke and Pepsi make products we enjoy. As an investor, I prefer the Coca-Cola Company. One reason is the amount of FCF generated for every sale. Since Coca-Cola has a combination of a special brand advantage, large scale cost of production advantage, and a global network distribution advantage, we could say that it has three moats around its economic castle.

Warren Buffett also commented on the competitive arena of selling insurance. He said, "Insurers will always need huge amounts of reinsurance protection for marine and aviation disasters as well as for natural catastrophes. In the 1980s much of this reinsurance was supplied by 'innocents' - that is, by insurers that did not understand the risks of the business - but they have now been financially burned beyond recognition." In the world of marketing super-catastrophe insurance, Buffett said Berkshire Hathaway enjoys a significant competitive advantage because of its premier financial strength.

COMPETITION SIMPLIFIED AND DEMYSTIFIED

How does practical competitive advantage tie in with current academic thought? In his book, "Competition Demystified", Bruce Greenwald of Columbia University presented a new and simplified approach to business strategy. The conventional approach to strategy taught in business schools is based on Michael Porter's work. In Porter's model, students can get lost in a sophisticated model of a business' competitors, suppliers, buyers, substitutes, and other players.

Greenwald warns us to not lose sight of the big question, "Are there barriers to entry that allow us to do things that other firms cannot?" Then, after establishing the importance of barriers to entry, Greenwald and Kahn argue that there are really only three sustainable competitive advantages; 1. Supply. A company has this edge when it controls an important resource: A company may have a proprietary technology that is protected by a patent. 2. Demand. A company can control a market because customers are loyal to it, either out of habit - to a brand name, for example - or because the cost of switching to a different product is too high. 3. Economies of scale. If your operating costs remain fixed while output increases, you can gain a significant edge because you can offer your product at lower cost without sacrificing profit margins.

Wal-Mart has shown its power in scale, and Charlie Munger put it this way: "Kellogg's and Campbell's moats have also shrunk due to the increased buying power of supermarkets and companies like Wal-Mart. The muscle power of Wal-Mart and Costco has increased dramatically."

According to Professor Greenwald, the value of such a strong brand barrier can be quantitatively estimated. It is about equal to its "difficult for competitor to match" reproduction costs.

In order to insure success, the operation of these good businesses must continue to be in the hands of first-class, able, trustworthy, and experienced managers. Focus on whether these competitive advantages are due to power in demand, supply, or economies of scale. However, in this book, we simplify this even more into "cost" and/or "special" advantages. Then, we discuss our impressions of whether their moats can endure over time.

Warren Buffett and Charlie Munger look for companies that have a) a business they understand; b) favorable long-term economics; c) able and trustworthy management; and d) a sensible price tag. They like to buy the whole business or, if management is their partner, at least 80%. When control-type purchases of quality aren't available, they are also happy to simply buy small portions of great businesses. Buffett said that it is better to have a part interest in the Hope Diamond than to own all of a rhinestone.

The dynamics of capitalism guarantee that competitors will repeatedly assault any business 'castle, that is earning high returns. Buffett and Munger believe that a great business must have an enduring 'moat' that protects its excellent returns on invested capital. Strong barriers such as being the low cost producer (GEICO, Costco) or possessing powerful world-wide brands (Coca-Cola, Gillette, American Express, IBM, Kraft) are essential for sustained success.

Since business history is filled with companies with weak and temporary moats, the criteria of "enduring moat" caused Buffett and Munger to rule out companies in industries prone to rapid or continuous change. So, they avoid investing in technology companies. The chapter on IBM will explain why they recently invested in this technology related information solutions business.

Charlie Munger said, "How do you compete against a true fanatic? You can only try to build the best possible moat and continuously attempt to widen it."

THE WONDERFUL BUSINESS IS SEE'S CANDIES

See's Candies taught Buffett and Munger much about the evaluation of franchises. Both men admit that they have made significant money because of the lessons they learned at See's. See's is the wonderful business.

In their talks and writings, they refer to a great business as a "franchise" or a "wonderful business." Buffett wrote: "An economic franchise arises from a product or service that: (1) is needed or desired; (2) is thought by its customers to have no close substitute and; (3) is not subject to price regulation. The existence of all three conditions will be demonstrated by a company's ability to regularly price its product or service aggressively and thereby to earn high rates of return on capital. Moreover, franchises can tolerate mismanagement. Inept managers may diminish a franchise's profitability, but they cannot inflict mortal damage."

Buffett and Munger respect able and trustworthy managers. As you read about these 70 great businesses, think about the product or service that: (1) is strongly desired; (2) has no close substitute and; (3) has pricing power. As Buffett said, "A moat that must be continuously rebuilt will eventually be no moat at all. Additionally, this criterion eliminates the business whose success depends on having a great manager."

FOR FUTURE MANAGERS

While this book will help readers learn more about enduring competitive advantages, here is a little reminder about Buffett and Munger's contribution to behavioral finance. It was the subject of my first book, "The Four Filters Invention of Warren Buffett and Charlie Munger." Their four filters innovation helps us all find better investments: "Understandable first-class businesses, with enduring competitive advantages, accompanied by able and trustworthy managers, available at a bargain price."

If you have home run hitters, let them swing for the fences. Berkshire Hathaway is a collection of businesses that were picked for their unique economic advantages. Most of them are run by able and trustworthy managers. So, appreciate them and remember that the goal is not growth, but it is "growth in intrinsic value per share."

NOTES:

www.ingramcontent.com/pod-product-compliance
Lightning Source LLC
Chambersburg PA
CBHW021925170526
45157CB00005B/2188